Middleton Public Library
7425 Hubbard Ave
Middleton, WI 53562

COLE SPROUSE

FAMOUS ACTOR

KATIE LAJINESS

BIG BUDDY POP BIOGRAPHIES

Big Buddy Books
An Imprint of Abdo Publishing
abdobooks.com

abdobooks.com

Published by Abdo Publishing, a division of ABDO, PO Box 398166, Minneapolis, Minnesota 55439. Copyright © 2019 by Abdo Consulting Group, Inc. International copyrights reserved in all countries. No part of this book may be reproduced in any form without written permission from the publisher. Big Buddy Books™ is a trademark and logo of Abdo Publishing.

Printed in the United States of America, North Mankato, Minnesota.
102018
012019

THIS BOOK CONTAINS RECYCLED MATERIALS

Cover Photo: Angela Weiss/Getty Images.
Interior Photos: Album/Alamy Stock Photo (p. 15); Bryan Bedder/Getty Images (p. 17); Frederick M. Brown/Getty Images (p. 6); Jamie McCarthy/Getty Images (p. 27); Kevin Winter/Getty Images (pp. 13, 25); Maureen Donaldson/Getty Images (p. 9); Michael Kovac/Getty Images (p. 19); Mike Coppola/Getty Images (p. 29); RGR Collection/Alamy Stock Photo (p. 11); Richard Shotwell/AP Images (p. 5); Robin Marchant/Getty Images (p. 21); Stories In Light/Shutterstock.com (p. 23).

Coordinating Series Editor: Tamara L. Britton
Contributing Series Editor: Jill M. Roesler
Graphic Design: Jenny Christensen, Cody Laberda

Library of Congress Control Number: 2018948445

Publisher's Cataloging-in-Publication Data

Names: Lajiness, Katie, author.
Title: Cole Sprouse / by Katie Lajiness.
Description: Minneapolis, Minnesota : Abdo Publishing, 2019 | Series: Big buddy pop biographies set 4 | Includes online resources and index.
Identifiers: ISBN 9781532118036 (lib. bdg.) | ISBN 9781532171079 (ebook)
Subjects: LCSH: Sprouse, Cole, 1992- --Juvenile literature. | Actors--United States--Biography--Juvenile literature. | Television actors and actresses--Biography--Juvenile literature. | Suite life of Zack & Cody (Television program)--Juvenile literature.
Classification: DDC 782.42164092 [B]--dc23

CONTENTS

SUPERSTAR ACTOR 4

SNAPSHOT 5

FAMILY TIES 6

EARLY YEARS 8

SEEING DOUBLE 10

BIG BREAK 14

COLLEGE EDUCATED 18

RIVERDALE 20

AWARDS 24

GIVING BACK 26

BUZZ 28

GLOSSARY 30

ONLINE RESOURCES 31

INDEX 32

SUPERSTAR ACTOR

Cole Sprouse is a talented actor. He began his **career** as a child. While in his 20s, Cole starred in the hit TV show *Riverdale*. Fans around the world love watching him act!

SNAPSHOT

NAME:
Cole Mitchell Sprouse

BIRTHDAY:
August 4, 1992

BIRTHPLACE:
Arezzo, Italy

TELEVISION SHOWS:
The Suite Life of Zack and Cody, The Suite Life on Deck, Riverdale

FAMILY TIES

Cole Mitchell Sprouse was born in Arezzo, Italy, on August 4, 1992. His parents are Melanie and Matthew Sprouse. He has a twin brother, Dylan. Cole is 15 minutes younger than his twin.

DID YOU KNOW?
Cole was named after jazz singer Nat King Cole.

When they were young, Dylan *(left)* and Cole *(right)* went to movie openings with their mom.

WHERE IN THE WORLD?

EARLY YEARS

The Sprouse family moved to California when the twins were four months old. Four months later, Cole and Dylan starred in their first TV **commercial**.

The boys were on the TV show *Grace Under Fire* from 1993 to 1998. The two actors played one character named Patrick.

DID YOU KNOW?
Cole started snowboarding when he was only four years old!

The twins appeared in all 112 episodes of *Grace Under Fire*.

SEEING DOUBLE

Twins are often **cast** for many child **roles**. Laws limit how many hours a child can work on set. A film shoot may last longer than a child can work. So, each twin works part-time and shares the role of one character.

Cole and Dylan appeared in the 1999 film *Big Daddy* with actor Adam Sandler *(right)*. *Big Daddy* earned more than $235 million worldwide.

Cole and Dylan grew up in front of a camera. At seven years old, Cole earned his first **role** without Dylan. He played Ross' son Ben on the hit TV show *Friends*. Cole was going to be a superstar!

Cole *(left)* was a member of the *Friends* cast for three seasons. The show was on TV for ten years!

BIG BREAK

The brothers' big break came in 2005. They starred in *The Suite Life of Zack and Cody*. This was the first time Cole and Dylan played separate **roles**.

Cole played the character Cody Martin. And Dylan played Zack Martin. In the show, the twins lived in a hotel with their mother.

The *Suite Life of Zack and Cody* was on Disney Channel for three seasons.

The twins continued their success with the Disney show *The Suite Life on Deck*. From 2008 to 2011, this **spin-off series** took Zack and Cody on an adventure at sea.

In 2011, the two starred in *The Suite Life Movie*. The film was based on their popular show.

The twins appeared in ten different shows playing the Martin brothers.

COLLEGE EDUCATED

After high school, Cole and Dylan went to college. They **graduated** from New York University at age 22.

Cole did not go back to acting right after college. Instead, he **focused** on **archeology**. He also became a talented **photographer**. His photos have appeared in popular magazines.

In his free time, Cole loves to play video games.

RIVERDALE

After five years away from acting, Cole was not sure he wanted to act again. But soon, a new opportunity came along.

He **auditioned** for the teen show *Riverdale*. It is based on the *Archie* comic books. Characters Archie, Betty, Jughead, and Veronica are part of the show.

DID YOU KNOW?
The TV show *Riverdale* was filmed in Vancouver, British Columbia, in Canada.

First, Cole tried out for the role of Archie. But he chose to play Jughead Jones instead.

Cole joined the **cast** of *Riverdale* in 2017. He played Jughead Jones, a smart student who loves to eat. The character is also a talented artist. Jughead often wears a hat in the show, just like the comic book character.

DID YOU KNOW?
Cole often posts his photos on social media like Twitter and Instagram.

Jughead narrates the show. His voice introduces viewers to the main characters and the story line.

AWARDS

Throughout his **career**, Cole has been **nominated** for many **awards**. And he has won many of them.

In 2009, Cole was nominated for the Kids' Choice Award for Best TV Actor. But he lost to his brother Dylan!

In 2018, he was nominated for a Saturn Award. This award honors science fiction movies and TV shows.

In 2017, *Riverdale* won seven Teen Choice Awards! Cole took home the award for Best TV Actor in a Drama.

GIVING BACK

DID YOU KNOW?
Cole and Dylan traveled to Japan in 2013. There, they supported American society and education.

No matter how busy he is, Cole always takes time to give back. Over the years, he has found fun ways to give to **charities**.

He and Dylan taught **elderly** people to play video games. And he made milkshakes to help the Ride a Wave **Foundation**. The foundation helps kids with special needs.

Cole and *Riverdale* cast member Lili Reinhart attended the 2018 Met Gala in New York City, New York. The Met Gala raises money for the Metropolitan Museum of Art.

BUZZ

Cole's fame continues to grow. In 2018, he finished season two of *Riverdale*. And the next season is in the works. His **future** looks bright. Fans are excited to see what is next for Cole!

DID YOU KNOW?
Cole is set to star in the romantic movie *Five Feet Apart*.

Cole and the stars of *Riverdale* talked to fans at the 2017 Comic-Con in San Diego, California.

GLOSSARY

archeology a science that deals with past human life and activities as shown by objects (such as pottery, tools, and statues) left by ancient peoples.

audition (aw-DIH-shuhn) to give a trial performance showcasing personal talent as a musician, a singer, a dancer, or an actor.

award something that is given in recognition of good work or a good act.

career a period of time spent in a certain job.

cast to assign a part or role to. It is also the characters or people acting in a play or story.

charity a group or a fund that helps people in need.

commercial (kuh-MUHR-shuhl) a short message on television or radio that helps sell a product.

elderly somewhat old.

focus (foh-Kuhs) to give attention to.

foundation (faun-DAY-shuhn) an organization that controls gifts of money and services.

future (FYOO-chuhr) a time that has not yet occurred.

graduate (GRA-juh-wayt) to complete a level of schooling.

nominate to name as a possible winner.

photographer a person who takes photographs especially as a job.

role a part an actor plays.

series a set of similar things or events in order.

spin-off a television program, movie, book, etc., that is based on characters from another television program, movie, book, etc.

ONLINE RESOURCES

Booklinks NONFICTION NETWORK
FREE! ONLINE NONFICTION RESOURCES

To learn more about Cole Sprouse, visit **abdobooklinks.com**. These links are routinely monitored and updated to provide the most current information available.

INDEX

Archie (comic book) **20**
awards **24, 25**
Big Daddy (movie) **11**
California **8, 29**
Canada **20**
charities **26, 27**
Comic-Con **29**
Disney **15, 16**
family **6, 8**
Five Feet Apart (movie) **28**
Friends (television show) **12, 13**
Grace Under Fire (television show) **8, 9**
hobbies **8, 18, 19**
Italy **5, 6**
Japan **26**
Jones, Jughead **20, 21, 22, 23**

Metropolitan Museum of Art **27**
Nat King Cole **6**
New York **27**
New York University **18**
Reinhart, Lili **27**
Riverdale (television show) **4, 5, 20, 21, 22, 23, 25, 27, 28, 29**
Sandler, Adam **11**
social media **22**
Sprouse, Dylan **6, 8, 11, 12, 14, 16, 17, 18, 24, 26**
Suite Life Movie, The (movie) **5, 16**
Suite Life of Zack and Cody, The (television show) **5, 14, 15**
Suite Life on Deck, The (television show) **5, 16**
United States **26**